BLUEBIRD
and Other Poems

BLUEBIRD
and Other Poems

Ranjita Nayak

Translated by
**Jayanta Mahapatra
Sangram Jena**

BLACK EAGLE BOOKS
2019

BLACK EAGLE BOOKS
USA address:
7464 Wisdom Lane
Dublin, OH 43016

India address:
E/312, Trident Galaxy, Kalinga Nagar,
Bhubaneswar-751003, Odisha, India

E-mail: info@blackeaglebooks.org
Website: www.blackeaglebooks.org

First International Edition Published by
BLACK EAGLE BOOKS, 2019

Bluebird and Other Poems
by Ranjita Nayak
Translated by **Jayanta Mahapatra & Sangram Jena**

Original Copyright © **Ranjita Nayak**
Translation Copyright © **Jayanta Mahapatra & Sangram Jena**

All rights reserved. No part of this publication may be reproduced, stored in a retrieval system, or transmitted, in any form or by any means, electronic, mechanical, photocopying, recording or otherwise without the prior permission of the publisher.

Cover & Interior Design: Ezy's Publication

ISBN- 978-1-64560-052-7 (Paperback)
Library of Congress Control Number: 2019957591

Printed in United States of America

Acknowledgements

I express my sincere thanks to Professor Jayanta Mahapatra and Sri Sangram Jena, who translated these poems from Odia to English, the editors of Indian Literature and The Telegraph etc. for their help and co-operation.

I also express gratitude to Black Eagle Books for this publication.

- Ranjita Nayak

CONTENTS

JAYANTA MAHAPATRA

Circus	11
Sweeper	13
Discovery	14
Mango Blossoms out of Season	16
Strange River	18
So Many Times, Just Like this	20
The Emperor Chitragriba	22
The Bird that has flown	24
Preventive Measures	26
The Corpse Bearer	28
Relationship	30
Not a Toy	32
Zoo	35
Temple Building	36
Unsaid	38
Whose Soft Footfalls are these?	39
Blue Bird	40
Where are you?	42
River	43
Dhauli	44
All Plays have been over before	46
Boat	47
The Flag	49
Shoulders	51

SANGRAM JENA

Address	55
Hypnotism	57
A Tiny Piece of Land	59
My Story	61
The River and the Boat	63
The Dream – 1	65
The Dream -2	66
I don't want to see a dream today	67
Faith	69
The Inner Truth	71
The Search	72
Halt for Sometime	74
Metamorphosis	76
A Poem	78
The Answer	80
Parallel Lines	81
She sits there	83
Quest	84
Identity	85
A Journey	86
The Veda	88
Still Excited	90
The Artist	91
Fort_Barabati In Ruins	92
Diary	94
A Fight	96
Rain	98
The Poetry of Darkness	99
Boatman's Song	100

Translated by

JAYANTA MAHAPATRA

Circus

Look, Ma!
how I have changed.
No more do I
obstinately insist to visit the circus.
You must be remembering my childhood.
How I forgot hunger and thirst
when the circus came to town.
At night, in my sleep I dreamt
how the ringmaster made the tiger and bear,
lion and jackal, perform their tricks
at times in the open, cracking his whip,
or inside the closed cage at others.
In my excitement, I'd clap with joy,
or bare my teeth and taunt those beasts
who responded obediently to gestures.
Suddenly I'd awake
and find the tents had already been removed,
the field deserted;
only a line stretched towards me
resembling a line of moving ants.

Look, Ma!
the dark serpent of fate
has coiled itself around the sacred basil,
ferocious animals crowd inside

that tender green heart you gently nourished.
Bruised, wounded,
listening to their commands,
I go on performing, circus-like,
Ma! look,
how I have changed.

■

Sweeper

Why are you in such a hurry?
Wait a little while,
daybreak is still far away.
My little son is fast asleep
after his offerings
to his forefathers on the night of
Diwali.

My precious heritage
lies scattered like pearls
here and there,
the sparklers of faith
are wet with dew.

Just wait a little,
let my little son be awake.
With his tiny fingers,
he will gather
the shiny pebbles from the seashore,
the mottled shells and conches,
and save for the depth of darkness
the half-burnt sparklers
after drying them in the sun.

Wait a little while, Sweeper,
daybreak is still far away!

Discovery

Leave evil spirits out;
even as a child, shadows gave me a fright.
And when one glances
at the village cremation ground,
the eyelids close on their own.
That's why Grandmother
had tied a talisman around my arm.
Nevertheless, the day
I began searching for the place where I lived,
the talisman got lost as I bathed in the river,
and my eyes opened on their own.
My graves lay spread out almost everywhere,
not an inch of space was left bare.
Some destroyed graves were all earth,
some even a thousand years old.
Few were covered with moss,
and lime oozed out of some.
Then too, some were, brand new,
with the mason plastering some.

Wandering around,
I found my corpse lying somewhere.
Rotting, emitting foul smell.
Impossible to breathe there.
A police constable was driving away

jackals and mongrels as he sat on guard.
I heard there might be a post mortem,
and justice administered.
I wanted to laugh out loud.
Smiled a little.
The entire earth shook.

The corpse wasn't mine
when one gave a close look.
The watchman's dead body lay there.
What fear do I have?
I am a fear myself.
And then I felt
I had found the place I lived in.

Mango Blossoms out of Season

Not only one, but seven
boys and girls
leap into my sari's loose end,
like fresh blooms from the tree
at one single call.
Laughing, they cling to the shoulders
and romp and play piggyback.

The sorrowful mind of this mother
wiping the royal stables
returns from that far-off land,
the withering tree bursts into flower.
Heaven is here at arm's reach.
Nothing turns out different,
Rambha and Menaka,
Parijata and Airavata –
So much so, the Pitcher of nectar,
together, all create a din
inside silence.

Feet inside the earth,
the rock gazing upward
from neck-deep water

finds the sky missing
from its place.
Fallen into the water long back,
thrashing its tail like a fish.
The eyes close at such a sight
in total disbelief:
Is it the sky
or a fish?

Is she the bald-headed one
wiping the stables
or a queen of the palace?

Strange River

How strange is that river!
Always dry and hard in its heart;
Yet, when you shift the sands aside,
appears rill after rill of sparkling water!

Really, how strange is that river!
Overflowing the banks, crossing road and fence,
it runs quietly,
no one knows where and when.

Fields and gardens, shrubs and trees,
villages and low-lying slums,
are shaken by its flow,
day and night, without respite,
without a sound.

When one wishes for a drop from heavens,
the entire heavens crash on one's head;
the *Ganga* rushes down the sage's braid
and flows past the Mount *Kailasa*,
awakening hill and jungle, arid land;
flurries of laughter swirl everywhere
and silence's spell is broken.

At other times,

when one asks for just a little,
one doesn't get anything
even the size of a needle point.
Light and wind vanish,
so much so that a full-wombed river
turns dry and hard,
or else becomes ice, without a ripple.
And the autumn sky, like a shady path,
simply a sign
trembles the rib-cage.

So Many Times, Just Like this

Not once
but often.
Many a time, I've heard
his footsteps.
I've felt his breathing
many times,
when I am alone.
So much so
that on some days,
hearing his call
I am wide awake;
then, however I try
much to put myself to sleep,
singing a lullaby
sleep evades me.
My body is pricked by thorns,
a bed of arrows.

I get up from my bed,
open the door and find
nobody there,
just darkness everywhere.

Earth's dense jungle of darkness
is eternally green.

Tall trees
touch the sky,
full of flowers in the sky.
A sky of flowers.

The flowers shake in the breeze
and stare at the earth,
the runaway hides in the thick bush.
My wings flutter.
The runaway gropes around
for a sparkler,
perhaps, I might find him
at arm's reach.
A whistle sounds in the distance.

Just this moment
the train must have left
the railway station
for some unknown kingdom.
I am flustered
at my own ineptness.

■

The Emperor Chitragriba

The emperor is a prisoner.
Imprisoned, this old king
in a house of stone.
On the other side of the wall
the season has changed,
earth's colours have changed too,
a new sun and new clouds
and such a change that even
hill and stream, tree and sea
take on a new look –
new scent wafts through the air.

A new king rules the jungle.
In his mask of blood,
the new king hunts around,
roaring as he leaps,
as all sounds keep floating
through a soundlessness –
one at a time sometimes,
bound together raft like at other times,
sweeping everything by.

If you put your ears to it
you can hear that sound
detect its scent

and see the carnivorous plant
beside the wall
with insects of all kinds
swarming about in their helplessness.

And I lose consciousness from time to time.
In the trembling of my heart
grows the rustling of an unknown fear.
Under my soul of blood and tears
are persistent sobs.
Imprisoned in his house of stone
Chitragriba:
defenceless low-lying cloud!

The Bird that has flown

It was between
you and me.
The mute hour,
the daylight,
night's darkness
were all witnesses.

You said
you'd never leave.
And if you leave,
you would return soon
before the shadows darkened
before the tree you planted
flowered and burst into fruit
in our garden.

No clouds in the sky
no gales on earth
nothing to stop you
from coming here –
still you do not come.

After you leave
I watch the tit singing its tune
day after day,

cleaning its beak, dipping
into the soft shoots
of that tree.

Are you the same bird?
Or are you that vast nothingness
tenderly clasping the tree?
Or that flitting mottled butterfly?
If you aren't, are you the buds
that have sprung on the tree?
To blossom into flower
then fruit and ripen
when the sun rises tomorrow?

■

Preventive Measures

There's no action left
in my body,
no preventive measure,
nor can I transcend myself –
Yet,
I am neither inert
nor a lifeless being.
Somewhere,
the moon has come to a stop,
caught as it were;
there itself
it rises and sets,
in a life of inaction.

Why does this happen?
Who plucked everything
from my boughs. . .
squeezing the juices out,
making prisoner forever
all possibilities of fruit and flower?
Singing lullabies,
stroking, calming the upset nerves
to sleep, but why?

How did this sea quieten,
the beach and casuarinas grove
turn into spirits of the dead?
How did this deep intimacy
cool down,
the string of relationship
tear into shreds?

And mind and body
fall apart?
Is it a mere movement
from time to time,
a testimony to inertness
from life unchanged through the ages?

If it isn't
is it just a matter
of carrying rocks along a blind alley,
or just a wish
to fly like a child's kite
with the reel of thread
in another's hands?

The Corpse Bearer

The funeral ground is far away.
Like a beast of burden,
the corpse bearer walks ahead
step by step.

Countless corpses on his shoulders
enmeshed as though in a cobweb,
their spindly legs and hands
hanging in strands
asleep on his shoulders
a long long time.

One and all are known to him.
A few even are very close –
The thick light and the blue moon in the sky
and the twisted blue braids of moonlight
are quite intimate with him –
His joys and sorrows, his relationship
bound to him
with twine soaked in blood and tears.

Today, he is a corpse bearer.
All others, each one of them
is a corpse upon his shoulder.
Unbreakable toys all,

that cannot be destroyed, burnt or sunk
or made to rot inside a grave.
Endless time just rides upon his shoulders.

Once in a while, they come alive
stretching their limbs,
to look around for light and air,
their subdued murmurs
swimming about in the wind –
Many questions, one after another,
suddenly come rushing in
like waves of the sea.

Yet the man who can answer
is like a lifeless tree lying motionless,
without look or voice,
because he himself
is a living corpse and corpse bearer.
His funeral ground is far away.

Relationship

You are the navel's lotus-centre
and I the circumscribing circle.
More than familiar,
we are acquaintances for a long time,
It's not that we have never
known each other.

In this enchanted valley,
where flowers bloom black and white
shadows of men and flocks of sheep
here in a gardener's world
I am held a helpless Prisoner,
an autumn breeze.

This ocean's roar enters the world
and yet nothing can be heard
as some sound in a room of glass
returns, having moved aimless.
Along the turnings of the mind –
History hides, the pyramids tumble
along with the achievements of ages.

A time of stone
wanting to save itself
and I, seek some refuge –

I look at the sky and earth.
But neither earth nor sky is seen
A pall of mist hangs everywhere
from the closed room, shards of plaster
fall down.

From some far-away place
a distant tune on the flute, the sound
of ankle-bells
bring a trembling to the heart;
It's not that I have never known it.
Beyond the word of sound, sound's phantom deer
takes wild leaps from forest to forest
along the hills,
losing herself in someone else
without losing herself.

The night's dew shines
on wilted leaves.
The mind, thrilled,
shakes itself and sits up
each prop of trust and faith
helps to straighten
the falling body and mind.

This relationship between us
is not new at all.

Not a Toy

A toy is bloodless.
A toy has no blood, no flesh,
it doesn't have the usual excitement,
neither hope nor desire,
a toy has none of these, nothing at all.

Its body is made of dry wood
and torn cloth, ornamented
in many ways, it marks rhythm,
dancing away under the puppeteer's fingers.
The heavy monsoon rains
wash off all guilt and trash.

Delight brims over,
applause is heard,
handful of laughter
scatter and fall everywhere
like sparks from a firecracker.

Its companion is a tyrant.
With the sea's thirst,
its cruel friend builds

hurricanes of tyrannical rule.
Every limb tore to pieces,
crushed to death with a stone
in Kansa's prison.

The body, discoloured in fire and smoke.
The wingless butterfly,
the hearts writhing in agony
long lines of ants on the earth.

Soon, one sees the toy
attired in a garment of flesh.
Now, it plots with the heat of blood
at times murmuring
with some tuneless melody.

Or, with a mountain spring or river
Sometimes, with the breeze
and then too with a bird
sweeping past in the skies
or with the sun
peeping through a chink in the clouds.

Who knows what it plots?
The next moment
hundreds of toys assemble in a fair
here and there in the streets.
Under their eyes
is the heat of burning fire,
even tall trees wilt and wither.
With feet of iron
the earth trembles,
sky, earth, water and wind

quiver in the slogans of revolt.
The seed asleep under the earth
awakes, thrusting for light and air.

The simple, plain face of the toy
appears a stranger,
taking on another face,
as though it is not a toy any more.
A cheetah, whose prey has been
snatched away from its mouth
some time before,
sits, striking its tail on the ground.
The cheetah waits for its opportunity
as it sits and strikes its tail.
It will wait for its chance,
capture its own rights
and write the history
of its life as it gambols around
in the dense forest.

Zoo

I wandered around and saw the entire zoo.
So many strange creatures,
green shrubs and creepers
many splendored scenes, in many hues –
those burrs got sewn in.
Sometimes, the waves of some strange sea
have come rushing in
to sweep one away without knowing.
Then again, have flung one on the beach,
sand crabs sink into the wet sand
waiting for the returning wave.
One holds on to an *anchal*
another holds someone's hand
tears have flowed
thorns have pierced the feet
and blood has flowed surely for someone.
Still, no one has been able
to hold on fully, at any time.

Enough,
one has wandered enough.
It is time now
for you to show me the way
to the lighted forest,
where no shadows ever fall
Or where illusion
does not haunt any more
anyone at any time.

Temple Building

From the day
the temple was built,
I walk around it
morning and evening,
every day, at dusk and dawn,
I walk around the temple.
Fire, air, south-west, north-east
I look carefully from every corner
from all ten directions.

I don't know what happens
but some flaw still remains
even when I build to perfection.
I am not satisfied. At times,
I remove a brick somewhere, somehow
Or insert another brick
in a different way,
The picture of the temple changes;
this goes on.

As the temple changes
the goddess's face is transformed.
The soul too changes
when the sword is placed on the ground.
Everything changes,
the offerings to the goddess,
lamp and incense,
everything.

Breaking and rebuilding goes on
in this manner
each day, only through words
the temple is built
and the icon
shaped inside the shrine.

Unsaid

I have thought of those so often.
Whenever I approach you,
you move away into the distance
like the horizon, every time.
I get enmeshed, tied down
in all the brambles and litter
of the world.

Bloodied hands and feet,
Ah, what excruciable pain!
I am free from it the next moment
gushing open like a monsoon stream,
I burst forth into open laughter.
As if nothing had ever happened
Or will ever take place.
It is like this, every time.
Really, what life is this?
What sort of death?
Just bobbing up and down
in these muddy waters all the time.

Whenever I approach you,
you move away into the distance
like the horizon, every time.

Whose Soft Footfalls are these?

Everything appears so very different.
Water and air, sky and earth
each one tastes different,
each has its own smell, its own view.
So different, each one.

Around us, the signature
from an unwritten hand.
Who comes down with soft slow steps?
Droplets of dew gleam like pearls
the white grasses smile, the earth changes.
What is that indigo line on the horizon?
Who comes?
Who is he, cosseting me, who pulls me close?
Then giving me kiss after kiss,
keeps on caressing me?
Ruffles the hair of the innocent infant
lying asleep in the ivory bed –
under whose embrace?
The shut door of consciousness opens
and a bud trembles
to open up into flower, petal by petal.
Someone is here, so close by,
and yet miles away.
Whose soft footfalls are these?

Blue Bird

I knew you would come,
surely you'd come.
Tomorrow, if not today,
along the blue of the sky,
rowing with your oars
like a blue bird.
Although I've planted banana trees at the door
to welcome you,
I haven't set up the ritual vessels,
I haven't kept parrots and mynahs
as pets in the courtyard
nor have I placed a silver plate
on the window-sill with food in it.

Simply because
I don't feel the need for it.
Dear blue bird of mine!
I have experienced both darkness and light
because of you.
I have tasted nectar, drunk venom
on the steps, both while going up and coming down,
suffering various pleasures and agonies
in my own being.

Opening doors and windows
I wait and look out today
for that moment when you would come
and with your touch
extinguish the sacred fire.
When you caress me with your tender wings
singing a lullaby,
I will then fall asleep
watching you with sleep-filled eyes –
without a care in my blue bed
like an angel in blue –
My dear blue bird!

Where are you?

What impatience is this
for a palm full of water,
for a burst of cool breeze
what restlessness!

From morning till evening,
from month to year,
this long wait for a garland of light
between seeing and unseeing
the intoxication to grope around
remains ceaseless, unending.

Where are you?
You aren't anyone's
and yet, belong to all.
Then, where does the clock's hand stop?
In heaven, in earth, or in hell?
In a point of sound or in a roar?
All is one.

In one too are many flows
Adam's bridge is perhaps
being built or being destroyed.
The Mahabharata is either beginning
Or coming to an end.
Just say:
What is that going on, then?

River

When one stands there
the melting flow of the river
can be partly seen.
Inside the limits of experience
can be read,
the view of the riverbank;
whatever melts in the heat
is not ice, but man;
whatever flows by
is not water, but life.

In the compassionate notes of the flute
the gaze swims through,
crossing thickets and shrubs and mounds
on the distant shore cradled by sandbanks,
the river lies ahead.

Our momentary relationships
would have gone back long since,
still one can decipher the river's destiny
from the blurred writing of snails and moss,
for nothing remains un-understood,
from the centre to the periphery.

When one stands there,
the sound of heavy rain
is heard from all around,
enveloping us,
the river, just the river.

■

Dhauli*

Nothing to view there,
yet the viewing never ends,
I just stand there transfixed.

In the cool monsoon rain
the green rice breaks in waves.
At the foot step of the hills,
time lies spread under the tree shades,
like a tired bear.
The emperor's sealed treasure chamber lies open,
when the morning's promise is surrendered
to the evening, what else is there?
Like a silent ascetic sits Dhauli,
perhaps the last view one will ever see.

Stooping to lift a handful of earth
time, started, begins to awaken.
Smell and touch and scene
mingle to become a tilak
on the forehead of a blade of grass.
Ritual time.

Moving away from a prayer's chant,
like a severed paper-kite
crossing field and grove, river and hill,

I pass by, as though looking for someone,
Is he a king, subject or obedient slave?
Or, a meditating sanyasi in a dim cave,
War or Peace?
Or ruins of sky, sea, wind or earth?
Time or life?
And whose key does it hold?

No one seems to be anywhere,
there is nothing here at all;
yet the search never ends.
I simply stand there transfixed;
Only life keeps on crossing the river *Daya*
carrying time quietly on its head.
Just that.

■

Place where the Kalinga war was fought, when Chandashoka was converted to Dharmashoka – an abode of peace.

All Plays have been over before

Even before a cloud crosses the sky
the peacock spreads its tail – feathered crown,
river and rill, hollow and pool fill to the brim
both banks overflowing in the flood.
Long before the touch
the shy *Mimosa* droops,
leaves trembling in shame.
Many hues smear themselves
on the tiny blossoms,
long before the petals
burst with their scents.
Before the arrow seeks out its target
the arrow pierces the heart,
the earth drips with warm blood,
the wounded dove
rolls on the earth in sheer pain.
Before the eyes are shut
all dreams are over,
the unconscious earth
lies asleep on summer's ground
without a protest.
Birds would have flown
before the eyes can open;
only empty boughs sway,
and the bare tree stares wide-eyed
holding on to its memories.
Before the play begins,
all plays are over.

Boat

The boat guards the ghat
even if the boatman is not there
at times on this bank or the other,
no one can break its journey
neither mountain nor ocean.
God or half-god, tiger and bear
sin and holiness, sun and rain
persons known and unknown,
none –
it ferries all across the river
even if water is there or not.

Sometimes, at odd hours
can be heard the poignant call
of a tired traveller who has lost his way,
from some far away place
beyond many births, urging it
to ferry him to the other bank:
'Wait a moment please!'
as the rain turns into a deluge
in the deepening dark.
And in the helpless call
is a mingling of sorrow and sighs,

and deep dark shadows,
the long wait of innumerable
faded dreams and much sadness.

Always ready to hear the call
is the boat, and also
ready to hear the river's song,
while the river hums on to
the tune of *Megha-Malhar*,
the traveller in the boat,
the dream inside the traveller
the river in the dream
and in the river, the boat
a black dot on the horizon.

■

The Flag

These days flags fly everywhere:
on temples, in play-grounds,
and market squares,
carried high in marches and processions.
Slogans for freedom and peace,
for friendship are voiced
the moment a flag is hoisted,
sugary words like drops of water
on ripe, red-hot molten iron –
In a distant field in new rain
a flock of sheep graze
on fresh grown grass, while dreams
keep on floating like
clouds in the sky.

Umbrellas are no more needed
to protect oneself
from sun and rain, cold dew,
every flag is a puppet
on each of the stairs leading to
the holy throne,
eloquent in its promise
to bring to our people
the pitcherful of nectar.

Head bowed, *Chemei Mallik*
sits, feeling the hot winds
blow under a flag,
and the icy gusts under another,
in one the season of leaf-fall
and the flash of lightening
in the other.
Which of the flags
would redeem him?
The white or the green,
the yellow or the scarlet?
The one on the temple top
or the one carried in the march?
Which place can
bring him redemption:
Kashi or *Varanasi*?

Everything appears to him
in the haze,
like the gloom of a grove
in a far-off village.
And in that darkness,
the past searches
for the shadow's soul.

The flag flutters on.

Shoulders

Because they couldn't stand
shoulder to shoulder,
they were not paired
to the plough.

The rains passed by,
with neither sowing
nor harvesting.

Look, the land lies fallow,
weeds grow everywhere.

Translated by

SANGRAM JENA

Address

After so many days
I have got the address of that place.
If you want to go,
then let us go to the forest
and become tress and mountains there.
It is better to be stone at once
like *Ahalya* and stretch the
hands from the earth to the sky
rather than to become stone gradually everyday.
If you want to go,
let us go to the forest.

We will make friendship
with the animals,
from them, we will learn
the way how to manage with
drinking water once a day
rather than drinking water
breathlessly in each moment.
We will recognize ourselves
washing our faces in the stream,
now let us go the forest.

Wearing a garland of aeons
and black and white flowers tucked in the braid

we will meet there an old female giant
who is putting her legs in the fire,
the key to unravel mysteries
tagged to the end of her *saree*,
that art of living known to her only.
We will listen stories from her,
wooing her, we will learn the hymn.
Let us go to the forest.

There in loneliness,
we will meet our ancestors,
know about them and understand them
as I am familiar with their language.
If you want, let us go to the forest,
after so many years,
I have found out
the lost address.

■

Hypnotism

Believe me,
I don't know the art of begging
with my knees bent.
Perhaps, for this reason
I have never asked for
anything from time,
neither the green wings
nor the golden feathers,
neither a port
nor a ship
loaded with dazzling diamonds and pearls.

I don't know
under what spell
I once asked time for
some lonely moments of *Gangasiuli*.
I showed some intimate documents of life
opening an old box
where palm leaf manuscripts
and stylus smeared with vermillion
preserved carefully
like the remains of
Mohenjo-Daro civilization
at the bend of the ancient river.

I carefully nurtured
the creepers of love
sometimes, spreading it on the roof
or hanging it in the void.
I tried to find out an alibi
to escape this breathless race.
Sometimes, I sat at a desolate place
or walked over a bed of fire,
spent sleepless nights
whispering to the moon and the stars,
scribbling on the wind
whatever occurred to me
raving like a lunatic.
Today, I try to find out
what was my mistake,
counting the stars in the sky
or begging before the time?

A Tiny Piece of Land

I roamed everywhere
inside and outside my home.
Nowhere I could find
a tiny piece of land
to plant the saplings of dream.

I thought that
this entire area is mine
like the kingdom of *Lanka*
totally secured with
high walls and closed gates.

Here, I can plant
anything of my choice
sow the seeds of rainbows
and plant green shoots somewhere inside.

I will put spring at one corner and
decorate sky with blue moon and stars.

I will donate the mountain facing me
to the clouds and peacocks.
But now I find
rat holes all around,
the terrorists rush inside

crossing the boarder
they sometime destroy
the railway lines by bombing
or take away someone as hostage
they go on capturing mountain
after mountains.

Nowhere a patch of land is visible
to keep my foot.
Only I am roaming
and roaming.

My Story

You accept it or not
I have taken you to be my teacher,
have resolved to give myself away.
I have taken out
all valuable robes from my body;
the sword from the scabbard
the cover from my eyes
the winter from mind
the hazy horizon from the heart
and hung them
on the tall tree branches
one by one.
Clearing a patch of the forest
I have made a gymnasium,
I have plastered the floor
with cow-dung mixed with lion's gesture,
have fixed the canopy and fences
with the timber of faith.
I have placed in rows clay figures
of ministers, generals, soldiers
and all the retinue
just like deaf and dumb pupils.

I have built with much care
your clay statue,
put life into it with the
chant of *mantrâs*.
I am learning the art of winning
by losing again and again,
and dreaming of completeness
amidst all incompleteness.

The River and the Boat

Day's light is waning
travellers crowding the
river bank,
a cacophony ensues
as storm clouds gather on the horizon.
Crossing the river,
they have to go a long way.
But the river ghat is empty,
the boat and the boatmen
nowhere in sight.
How do they cross
the brimming river?
How to get the boat?
The river and the boat,
the boat and the river ,
they are there or not
both the king and subjects
all gasping in the swirling waters
for breath
as always.
Yet, the boat is everywhere,
in the lofty heavens
and in earth's depths
in mountain crevices
beneath the desert sands,

on the island in the ocean
in dense forests
in the mind and thoughts
of the ascetics,
in the chanting of sages
in the sound of temple bells
in the voice of grand parents
the boat remains anchored
in waters, on the plains
everywhere,
at all times.

The Dream – 1

One day there was nothing
except the awakened dream.
Vishnu's eternal rest
in the ocean of milk
dreams all around
clusters of foaming milk,
dreams when you open your eyes
dreams when you shut them too.
Living and dying in dreams,
mango trees were laden with
bunches of fragrant flowers.
Something happens today
the dream loses its way
as if *Lakshman*'s
three prohibitory lines
are drawn for her.
fog burns the mango flowers
the smell of burning in the air
meting in the scorching sun
Gangashiuli's dreams flow down.
Dreams elude
calculations and formulae
whether you close the eyes
or keep them open.

The Dream -2

There was a time
when dream like a pole star
was guttering
a stray traveller, help in crossing
oceans, mountains, forest and deserts
escaping encounters from tigers,
bears and dangers on the way.

Today,
dream faults to lead this way
Kasatandi flowers
do not resist wind or rain,
unable to tolerate
earthly suffering
Ashwin's clouds in patches
float one end to the other.
Darkness swings empty branches.

A treacherous snake
sleeps curling near a bush
or is the crevice of stones.

I don't want to see a dream today

Earlier,
I used to see many a dream,
even I could see the dreams
in a half awakened state.
Dreams covered everything
no trace of drowsiness
was there in my eyes.

I swim in this void
like a fish,
swinging my arms,
I go up in the sky
leaving below houses and hills.
I still go up
touch the rainbow and the stars.

When I fly like a butterfly,
men become trees and creepers
flowers of many hues
bloom on its branches
my joy's sea of moon beam
crosses the shore
in a full-moon night.

Today, I don't like
to see dreams.
Now, dreams disturb my sleep,
cruelty licks the
innocent and gentle moon light.
I want to sleep,
go into a deep slumber.

Faith

Faith is a mirror
you can see the true image
of the world on it, so well.
Once it falls from the hand
it breaks into pieces,
you can't remake it
nor join them together
everything is erased at once
the name and the address.
Faith is a touch-me-not creeper
it bends at the raise of a finger,
closes even before you touch it.
Faith is a sacred *Gangasiuli*
blossoms stealthily in dark.
Among dense and coarse foliage,
at the slightest touch of sunrays
its butter-soft body melts.

Faith,
a tender feeling of trust
it is difficult to understand
and sometimes, hard to explain.
Faith can only be trapped by faith,
put in its own cage,
measured in its own scale,

a life of beauty can be lived by faith.
When faith stands in the witness box
a fertile green land turns dry and barren,
a blue line cannot be
drawn in the scorching desert,
the peacock does not spread its feathers
looking at
floating clouds.
Nothing is left
neither hope nor life
darkness, only darkness.

The Inner Truth

Everything was fine.
The river was flowing
the breeze was humming a tune
flowers were dancing
and nothing was missing.
At times a wisp of cloud only
covered the sun's face
breaking the defences
melancholia seeped in,
it went back like tidal wave
drenching a few moments.
How could I know
it augured the impending storm,
signalled catastrophe?
How could I know
you would go looking for the light
leaving the wife and son
by the wayside,
you would go searching for the starts
to light a lamp in deep darkness?
How could a dry leaf
floating in the stream know
the inner meaning
of the deep river,
the inner meaning of
the chant of 'OM'?

The Search

He told me,
Come, its getting late
let us talk for sometime
please sit down.

What are you looking for?
Have you lost your anklet, waist-band
or diamond nose ring in the forest?
There is no end to your search.

I said, Ok.
You could have known a tree
but not me !
I am nothing but a tree.
How can my search end?
Look,
my feet inside the soil
like roots of a tree.
My decayed body is blossoming
looking up for light and wind,
branches looking for birds
those will disperse seeds.

He replied,
you can search
like a tree
but do not become a bird
lest you would lose your way to come back
after flying in the sky,
with your wings open.

Halt for Sometime

How long you will continue?
Halt for some time,
listen,
somebody is calling you somewhere.

Somebody is calling you
from the other side of the *Meghanada* wall
or from below the Naval centre,
whose chanting is this?
Listen,
halt for some time.
Look,
how sorrowfully
this river looks at others.
It's mouth is covered with sand dunes
dead bodies of the tender dreams
are smeared all over with mud and dust
prow of a drowned ship is visible on water
a hawk is whirling in the sky,
sometimes a fish or a Canary at other times
flutter restlessly in its paw.

The heart of this
sleepy river shivers,
the earth is shaking

in somebody's dreaded roar.
The building are collapsing,
the old banyan tree is swaying
even if its roots are deep.
Listen, the sound of
a squirrel is in the hole of a tree trunk.
The waves digs away sands from
under the feet even if you stand firmly.
The moments are swollen like
balloons filled with feelings.
How long it will continue?
The pages of history open before you
like a bright morning.
Wait a while.
Listen,
perhaps somebody is calling you somewhere.

Metamorphosis

No more,
go back
you all my attendants
I have given my statement and
read out my last decision,
now you go back.
Like a beast carrying burdens,
I carry my commitments for eternity
from country to country
from planet to planet
on that inhospitable road,
time and again.
Imprisoned in mystery,
shivering tender life is tortured by endless pain,
life after life, death in a moment
all a routine affair.
Why this allurement?
What for this procession?
Do you think that
you can obstruct my way putting around me
a chain of human hands and
I will return as before?
Go back all my attendants
I have relinquished this diamond throne,
this bejewelled crown and all my ornaments.

I have distributed my energy, strength
my life and everything in my possession,
then why shall I make a retreat?
Go back you all my attendants.
Look,
how the trees and creepers shine
after being washed by a shower.
Look,
how it stretches out its hands
towards the sky.
Listen,
someone else's heartbeat from the
core of its heart intermittently.
No more,
go back, you all my attendants.

A Poem

That day,
I told him,
"don't call me *Kavita*
I have left writing poem".

He smiled.
Believe me, now-a-days,
I am not writing poems.
Look, could I tell
the story of my life
without reservation
in my poems?

So many times,
I have written these routine words like
"*Sa-re-ga-ma*",
that I got by heart in my childhood,
as the aboriginals
paint their walls routinely
in red and white.

How can I make you understand that
the river, trees, birds and wild animals
all enter into my heart
in a group, tormenting me,

some carry me in its current
someone drowns me
someone clings to me
someone makes me dumb.

In their company,
Sometimes, I become a river
Sometimes, a mountain, a tree
or a bird at other times.
How could I convince you
that the feet slips in sand
pulls it inside
to an abysmal depth,
crops get damaged in repeated cyclones
I am a fisherman's hamlet
on the sea shore.

I have decided not to write poems, instead
build a concrete house
on a piece of land lying vacant since long
and not vulnerable to cyclones.

Look,
I have drawn
the map of my house
with a beautiful garden, a broad veranda inside
and large windows to allow air and light.
Now, tell me how good is this idea?
Smilingly he replied,
What else is a poem?

The Answer

I have seen it.
Don't ask me,
how was that scene?

I have heard it.
Don't ask me,
what was that sound?

I know them,
Don't ask me,
how to reach the source?

Invisible
inexplicable
silence
is the answer
to all queries.

Parallel Lines

One day
he said, Go, Go.
leave this place.

Looking down,
while drawing
lines on the earth
with my nails
I replied, No, No.

Don't tell me to go ,
I have to write many poems.
Moving in the cycle of seasons
summer, winter and rains
arrived and disappeared,
leaves turned yellow and fell down
new leaves sprouted.
One day I told him,
now I will go.
No, No, he replied.

Don't leave, don't leave at all
your poem is half written.
Looking up at the sky
with a smile I said, No, No
don't tell me to stay
a poem is never complete.

Sometimes, the scorching sun
or cloud and mist at other time
fill the space between
these parallel lines.

She sits there

She sits there as it is,
under the tree
full of leaves
spreading the end of her *saree*
on the ground
like a stone sculpture
over the years.

You can see her sitting there
when sun rises
moon sets in
flowers bloom
and also when fruits ripe.

She sits there all along
when birds sing
and even after they fly away.

Taking her to be a beggar
whatever the passers-by donate
she does not touch them
nor replies to anybody's query.

She sit there, unmoved
like a deaf, dumb and blind one
spreading her *Saree*'s end.

Quest

Without thundering roar of *Bheem*
Duryodhan does not come out
of *pond Vyasa*.
The battle of *Mahabharat*
does not come to an end.
Door of a closed house
neither can be opened
without keys
nor darkness is dispelled.
Look at the
state of my mind !
Holding the key
in my left hand,
I search for it
throughout the world.
Is it the sunset
of my forgetting
or a sunrise
thereafter?

Identity

Whenever I ask your name,
you look at the flower
or at the moon,
you never tell me your name.

Whenever I ask
the name of your village
you look at
the other shore of the river
or this side of the river bank,
you never tell me
the name of your village.

Whenever I ask
for your address
you look up at the sky
or below to the earth,
you never give me
your address.

When I ask you
time and again
you tell me with a smile –
can't you identify a person
without knowing his name,
his residence, or address?

A Journey

I have left home
since long.
I know I have to reach
the destination
at a specific hour
or else I would miss many things,
skies, oceans, plants,
colourful birds and the seats of
many gods and goddesses,
even may lose many
auspicious moment of travelling.

On the uneven roads,
I walk with mountain *Gandhamardan*
on my one palm like *Hanumanta*
and holding tender *Gangasiuli* flowers
with the other.

I walk wearing an anklet on one foot to dance
while a mill-stone is tied to the other one.
My wings are smeared with caster oil
my steps are slowing down,
drops of sweats enter my mouth,
I don't have the strength
to walk fast like a tree ant.

I know, I am late
can't circle around the world
may be my journey
will remain incomplete
or else, I have to
move round the throne
like *Ganesha*, the remover
of all obstacles.

The Veda

In his sunken eyes
the path looked clearer today
the feeble watermarks
looked like pictures on a canvas.

Sitting alone on the veranda like a crow
why father was telling that day,
O! my dear daughter
leave me in my native village
where my umbilical cords
have been buried
and spread their branches like trees,
my walking stick
will never slip,
my feet will not tremble
there, the land of my ancestors.

In this polished marble house
my feet, my stick, all tremble
here the earth shakes
like a tree in the storm.

I hear a murmur
in my deaf ears,
a story I heard
in my childhood
in an winter evening,
is preserved as an unforgettable memory.

After my legs are broken
now, I could understand,
a deep current of a river
corrodes more inside
than what it erodes outside.

Still Excited

No rule exists.
How much powerful
your logic might be,
you lose the case
by the powerful argument
of your opponent's lawyer.
However perfect may be your maze
you cannot escape
Takshyaka's bite.
Amidst failures and defeats
you cannot die of your own accord.
Bhisma had to live on arrow bed
in the battle field of *Mahabharat*.
Not a patch of cloud in the sky
this mind like a green
crop field gets destroyed in a moment,
Chandashoka's sword
dazzles in the night's dense darkness.
Streams of blood, sweat
flow in river *Daya*.
Yet, life blooms
like a water Lily in the mud,
full of excitement
to listen to the *Raaga Megha-Malhar*,
and *Upagupta's* chanting of *"OM"*,
the seeds of non-violence and compassion,
coming from the depths of dark caves.

The Artist

In all ages,
the artist remains thirsty
as a traveller in desert.
He makes, breaks
again create, remain busy
as a child on the seashore.
The artist lost in himself
paints pictures, draws sketches
of dreams and memories.
The landscape, the scenes of
rains, spring and summer
all take shape by his tender touch.
A river flows down
coming from the dark crevice
of a mountain,
a wild being searching
for his roots
like the unfolding of clothes
layer by layer
that covers a nude body.
Yet, the life of an
artist is always miserable,
half drawn portraits, paint brush, colour
all lie scattered inside the room.
He groans in pain as if
bitten by a female black cobra
for his failure to paint
a real portrait of his beloved
till today.

Fort Barabati In Ruins

Whenever, I see
the ruins of *Barabati*
keep sleeping under the
bedspread of tenderness
like an innocent child.
To be in slumber
is its luxury,
I don't feel like
disturbing its sleep,
so each time I came back
from its Lion's gate.
The passion for sleeping
spreads from one person to the other
like heat in the iron.
Rising from sleep,
I promise that I will
wake it up from slumber
to know the missing links
of lost history.

Where can I get
a better guide than it?

It is the mute spectator
of the unknown history,
voices of joys and sorrows,
mysteries and memories
are preserved under its bosom.
The dust sits there
guarding it from all sides.
One day, when I reached there
I saw its bed scattered,
splashes of blood drops here and there.
Stunned, I saw all papers
and documents have been washed away
in an unknown stream.
Who knows?
Whether I can meet it again or not
in this birth,
I have to wait
for another cyclone or earthquake,
for how many rebirths
no one knows.

Diary

To sit like a crow,
I searched for a tree,
a branch bent with flowers.
I searched for a roof
and warm murmurs inside,
a narrow stream in the river
for my tiny dream boats.

I wandered
flying over the meadows and mountains
fields and forests, cities and countries
from house to house
branch to branch
heart to heart.
I searched for my dream land
flying breathlessly
defying heat, rain,
cold and dew.

I could not find
a tree full of leaves
everywhere, there was
the shadow of a tree.
I could not find a house,
everywhere, there was

the shadow of a house.
I could not find a river,
everywhere there was
the shadow of a river.
In this world full of shadows
there is no roof, no branch
nor the beginning of an auspicious morning.
Everything is a mirage,
a procession of defeated dreams
everywhere.

A Fight

All through the night
the mango tree in front of the house
was engaged in a deadly fight
with the storm
in the deep darkness
like a combating soldier
on the frontline.

In the morning
the tree was lying
on the road
with its branches spread all over
like a baby holding
his mother's belly.
Its roots were holding the soil,
a thick layer of new leaves and flowers
spread over the road
like a bedspread.
A broken ship lay scattered
on my mind's coast
all sealed valuables
covered with soft clay.
The soul bleeding by
a stroke of the woodcutter's axe.

The blank sky
the empty soil
intolerable pain inside,
slowly the seed is sprouting.

I could understand
there is no end to a fight.
It continues eternally
between two sides
somewhere or the other.

■

Rain

A heavy downpour today
streets and fields are not visible
ants, dirt all float
in rain waters,
Tuberoses by the side of the window
trembling in cold,
in today's heavy downpour.

The rain dances on the
back of the treeless hills,
on the body of the forest
on the chest of the Sea,
the wildfire is getting extinguished by rains.
The chirping of the baby birds
is not audible.
Heavy rain lashes *Kalahandi*,
a draught hit area.

A group of enchanted winged ants are flying outside
some rolling on the ground
with their wings severed.
The relation between
rain and the winged ants is never known
as we never find out
the forest roads during rainy season.
Today, there is a heavy downpour
also within me.

■

The Poetry of Darkness

What do I say about darkness?
Being a teacher,
you know it so well.
Darkness explores darkness
just as the root searches for water
in noiseless words.
Darkness beckons darkness
like a rabbit
it perks up its ears for the call
like a blind-man's stick
darkness leads darkness,
darkness melts into darkness
like water mingling with water.
You also know darkness never seeks light,
when it does,
a new era begins.
Vyas and *Valmiki* take birth
epics are written
like *Ramayana* and *Mahabharat*,
the seeking is what matters.

Boatman's Song

So many times
I have travelled on this path
even if I wished
to sit here for a while
in the evening or at noon
I have never found time
nor a shadow to sit under.
Every time, there is a hurdle.
I move along the countless orbits
completely submerged in myself.

Sometimes, the unruly current
of the river pulls me,
the *Banyan* tree stands
on its edge,
vultures and kites nestle
on its branches.

The tombs lying under the shadow of the tree
for generations
now threatened by the
leaping dark tongue
of this restive river.

The boatman's song is heard
crossing the boarders
of dream's circle.

The river does not look
at its bank
it does not keep account of
how much land has been eroded
or how much covered under sands.
It remains indifferent
to arrival and departure
of human beings.
It does not calculate
how much water
evaporated to the sky
and how much
the earth sucked.

The river
does not bother for anything,
always moves restless
like a Black Drongo.

www.ingramcontent.com/pod-product-compliance
Lightning Source LLC
Chambersburg PA
CBHW060500080526
44584CB00015B/1504